God in Winter

First published in 2015 by
The Dedalus Press
13 Moyclare Road
Baldoyle
Dublin 13
Ireland

www.**dedaluspress**.com

ISBN 978 1 910251 06 5

Dedalus Press titles are represented in the UK by
Central Books, 99 Wallis Road, London E9 5LN
and in North America by Syracuse University Press, Inc.,
621 Skytop Road, Suite 110, Syracuse, New York 13244.

Cover image: 'Frozen Fir Forest',
© Kamil Hajek / Dreamstime.com

The Dedalus Press receives financial assistance from
The Arts Council / An Chomhairle Ealaíon

God in Winter

Pádraig J. Daly

DEDALUS PRESS
DUBLIN, IRELAND

Contents

༆

For Sadhbh, Oisín, Jake, Sophie, Juliette,

Liam, Alannah, Lucas And Alex

Perspectives

1.

We are more than what seems —
Not bound to flesh's end,
But bred for a forever.

The littlest, most craven of us,
Walks out at evening,
Outshining the stars.

2.

Do not be overcome by the billions of us
Or be dismayed that our world is a speck among the stars.
Length and distance do not weigh for Him.
Creation folds to a zilch in His palm.

3.

Down through voiceless planets,
To where the human huddles in fissures above the water,
Comes the Word, for Whom all breadth
Is a bubble on the face of the sea.

Lucency

"There is no way of telling people that they are all
walking around shining like the sun".
— Thomas Merton

1.

Outside, smokers gather beneath a canopy.
The river, full of rain,
Is hurrying to sea.

At the far end of the bar,
They watch football.
No one scores. No one cheers.

Nearby, people drink companionably.
A man chuckles,
His old face made lucent by mirth;

And I grasp, in a clap,
How God has dreamt him
Through all the cycles of our evolving

And holds him in this shimmering now.

2.

Today we woke to snow.
Then, the freeze; and all the paths
Were plates of ice.
Rain came at noon,
Washing the meadows green.

Now the sun gilds a hem of cloud,
Crows, numberless, cacophonate on branches,
Seagulls stipple the lawn,
Dogs bark,
Waters gush and fall.

All through the park,
Men and women go by under trees,
Unaware of their own loveliness.

The Murder

It happened years before:
A young man, a sort of innocent,
Gunned down outside the chapel!

It was talked of still, shudderingly, when I was a boy.
People pointed out the place,
Lamenting the unholy slaughter.

What hammering conviction
Gives lives as small as his (or ours)
Such value?

Reflecting on Von Balthasar

1.

How can any of us,
There being so many of us,
Matter?

Yet each of us has woken once
To sunlight, sky, sounds of water;
And, like a child,

Returning for the first time its mother's smile,
Smiled back,
Knowing infinite cherishing.

2.

He came from under the trees
To a green meadow with cows grazing.
There were cornfields too,
Stretching brightly to the hill;
And water racing.

He knew friends would disappoint again,
Old companions cast him off,
Betrayal gash his heart;
But for now he lives, unfearing,
In the compassion of the sun.

3.

Midwinter.
Downriver, a million lighted offices:
Lives of hope, despair, workaday tragedy,
Washed all in God,

Who drew us first, from gases, fire and sands
(Through crawling slithering things),
To life;

And holds us closely.

4.

Light, creeping in over the city,
Swallows all our midget lights,
Bathing, with unutterable tenderness,
The fevered heart, the riven mind,
The tar-ry ways, the nooks we shelter in.

5.

Amid the rush and desperation of the city,
There are bright waterpools,
Where we can fold ourselves down into a perfect stillness
And wait till the ecstasy comes
As come, however fleet, it must.

Importance

Leaves shivering in the wind;
Somewhere, singing; puffball cloud:
Beyond them all, unthinkable space!

Across this ball of earth,
Billions of us
Moving beneath the sun!

Something more than us
Must make our importance.
Fathoming the What or Who buckles the mind;

Or the how of Your numbering every one of us-
Flesh stretched on bone! —
And loving us to the edge of rapture.

Lonergan: Recognising the Love

It is like swimming under the sea,
Becoming aware of a sunblast
Scattering orange slats through the water;

Or living in a room full of music,
Distinguishing once the pattern of a single flute
Gathering the wavering notes to a surge;

Or like feeling through your body
The intense blue of a cornflower
And the skinny reach-upward of grasses.

Creed

Six women and a crabbed man
Kneel before a monstrance.

I am old among them,
Grappling with my burden of untrust;

Yet knowing too that man is more than man
And this world more than this world shows.

Cars swish by on the roadway, a thrush sings,
A crazed woman moves newspapers from bag to bag.

The Ballyroan Baptism:
A Painting by Seán Keating

Christ to the front,
Solid as a baulk;
Above, the dove alighting;

People awed;
A child's eyes searching for a voice;
All held in a loose triangle:

For this and every chunk of world
Is hemmed by the Three;
And all our action is the carry-on of God.

Comprehension

1.

Walking the shore,
Tormented by the mystery of what is,
Augustine saw a boy baling the ocean into a pool,
Knew the folly of knowledge,
Knelt.

2.

We, who cannot comprehend the ocean —
Its rocks and stones and corridors,
Its gay cavorts with light —

Who cannot understand the earth —
Its birds, its crops,
Its skies —

Who cannot grasp
The outspin of the universe,
Nor plumb the turvy mind,

Try yet to fathom Who You Are.

3.

Vastness is not vast to You,
Who move through icy reaches, laughing,

Who hold universes like sand
In Your fingers.

.s shadow
ubs on the estuary mud,
is full,
ts flicker along the promontory,
screech:
 rld is held in contained ecstasy.

 lk under uncountable stars,
 are that space to You
 s as a speck;
And I and all my kind
Are kept here out of love.

2.

In this corner of the immensity,
Under climbing trees,
Far from our nearest star,

Let us live kindly with one another,
Knowing that, in some unnameable way,
Such small living matters.

3.

Outside it is dark.
Streetlamps along the river burn into the gloom.
The mist on my skin convinces me of Benevolence.

Everything

1.

Treep of dunlin, scent of lemon,
Fallen blossom fleeing before the wind,
Nuzzle of sheepdog, apple in the mouth,
Crunch of gravel:
The miracle of everything!

2.

The sea moves ever to shore,
Breaking down the shells,
Softening the contours of stones,
Making shards of glass innocuous,
Heaving a sparkling bounty onto land.

3.

A herring gull twists its head to eye me from the water,
A seal pants heavily.
A plane is labouring through the sky.
A boat going, a boat coming:
Feel how God, with warmth envelops the world.

4.

Take the grassy track behind the houses
To a green clearing away from every noise
But the noise of flies in hedges,

Noise of birds, noise of water.
Waiting there, let Him find you.

5.

The night is dark.
The stars are sleeping.
Listen to the rain!
It is God, loving the world.

Other

She sits in a window,
Sun in her hair,
Net curtains moving lazily behind her.

For this one moment, I glimpse perfection
And think how Other You must be,
Your beauty repeating everywhere.

Mist

All that week, I listened to tides brush the boats,
Turbulence of pebbles,
Screech of goose and waterbirds.

I never saw the mountains
That rose, sheer and suddenly from the lake,
Felt only a certainty of presence.

Rubble

A long avenue of elms,
Then a cobbled square,
Chimneys rising to frame the moon.

Gates and painted doors,
Streetlights in lines,
Granite walls holding back a river.

Beyond them all, the stars;
And, falling forever through emptiness,
Rubble of planets.

Wonder

1.

How small we are beneath the stars;
And out and out stretch planets
Through the emptiness:

But wonder stops short if God is not;
And nothing has reason to be marvellous.

2.

We flit through the world
Like authors of our own existence,
Full of an importance not ours,
Parading a glory we have not earned.

Is Ór nGlan

from the Irish, 12ᵗʰ century

He is pure gold, bright sunlight,
A silver vessel filled with wine,
An angel, heavenly wisdom,
He who does the King's bidding.

He is a bird ensnared,
A ship holed and sinking fast,
An empty cask, a wizened tree,
He who follows not the King's decree.

He is a scented branch, heavy with flower,
A butt of honey,
A healing, precious stone,
Who does the bidding of God's Son.

He is a barren husk,
A foul stench, a dying tree,
An apple branch that never flowers,
Who follows not the King's decree.

He who does God's Son's will
Is bright sun in Summer,
God's throne in paradise,
A glass vessel, catching light.

He is a horse pacing a meadow,
The man who is greedy for God's pleasure,
A chariot with reins of gold,
Carrying the chief triumphant home.

He is a sun that warms the heavens,
He with whom the King is pleased,
A blessed temple,
A shrine with gold finish,

An altar where wine is given,
Where many choirs are singing,
A chalice wine-filled,
White bronze, very gold.

Dreamers

1. Taormina

Above the fields and trees,
He has created a small paradise,
Diverting a stream, sowing drifts of blossom,
Painting walls and windows like a gypsy's cart.

He never takes time
To sit among flowers,
Listen to water:
The dream is all that matters.

2. Wicklow

Somebody, who knew he'd never live
To see them rise so gaunt and lovely, full of crows,
Above the empty Winter meadow,

Dreamt of those tall trees
And of us (unknown) who watch them, ravished.

3. Catania

With precise taps of hammer on pegs,
He is training tendrils of jasmine
Along a sunlit wall.

The leaves are soft: No flower has come:
But he dreams of white stars,
Laying scent along the dark.

Cunnigar

Crunching as a boy on razorshells,
Examining shoelace whorls on sands,
Racing into water,
I was waiting always
For the seas to wash me in
A pirate crate of treasure.

Back again,
Tide on ebb,
Sun falling on far-off breakers,
I know the sea itself
Was my treasure
And I carry its light forever.

Blown Leaves

Somewhere above this ball of earth,
There are vast calms.
Here there is nothing but the noise of stirred-up wind.

Dead leaves swirl past the window,
Borne upward for a time
To fall lightly again who knows where.

I imagine a man, sun returned,
Opening a door on a treeless street
To a yellow ecstasy of leaves.

Eggs

It was a place of pigeons fluttering.
A thrush tugged at a worm.
A solitary cloud boded rain.

In the middle of the field,
A giant chestnut was white with blossom.

A cyclist pushed against the hill.
Men gathered by the ruined factory
In faded overalls.

Behind a window,
Someone broke eggs into a pan.

Light

There is a place up here
Where they finish the long crossing of the mountain
And people leave their lamps behind
For new travellers going the other way to find.

Instead of diminishing,
The stock of light at either end grows larger.
Better lanterns have appeared,
With less fiddling with wick and oil.

Retreat

I left the leaping horses behind,
The vivid tents, the race of water,

The fathers taking photographs,
The mothers, after the ordeal, gasping for tea,

The sons jostling,
The girls, in billowing frocks, laughing across a bridge;

And found a way uphill
To a green square, where the gentle old

Gather in shafts of dying sun.

Terminal

The great windows look out on aeroplanes
Rising and returning.

Far away, a line of trees,
Green above the scorched grass;

And, through a gap, the red sun
Going down into the sea, protesting!

Afternoon

All kinds of things are happening:

A woman comes to a far balcony to water flowers.
A red blouse hangs high against the pale wall of her apartment
Like an emblem of the Sacred Heart.

A young girl wraps herself
In the smells of sun-bleached sheets.
A train in the valley tugs carriages of cantaloupes.

Pigeons take over the day,
Thankful for crumbs, eggshells, castaway fruit —
The harvest of our excess.

The Wooing of Étáin

from Tochmharc Étáine, 9th Century

Fairest Maiden, won't you come
To the land of wonders, land of song,
Where every head is primrose yellow
And snowy bodies are ever young.

No wealth is termed mine or yours there,
Black each eyebrow, white each smile;
Your eyes would joy to see our number
With cheeks a foxglove red on white.

Every purple hill is meadow.
The small birds' eggs would lift your soul.
Though you love the land of Fáil most dearly,
If you knew Magh Mel, you'd not come home.

Great-Grandchildren

for my father

I wish you could see
Your great-grandchildren thrive,
Exult in the din of them together:

The falls, the scrapes, the tears,
The kissing-better.

You would glory in their innocent cheek,
Naïve knowing,
Love for each and each overwhelming you!

Leaving the Party

for Sadhbh

Princess though you are, in First Communion dress,
Fresh from your parlay with Christ,

You are the little girl too,
Leaping from the windowledge

To wrap skinny arms round me tightly in goodbye.

Juliette

1. TADPOLE (AGED 2)

Like a tadpole
Darting every whichway through the water,
She is all about the room,

Stopping impishly
Before each besotted adult
Before she ducks again

And dives and parries
In her aqueous element.

2. HALLOWEEN (AGED 2 AND A HALF)

She is fearful of the grey witch in the hall,
Who cackles as she passes,
Whose eyes light with demonic glint,
Whose chair creaks, whose skirts rustle.

But perched high once more
In the sanctuary of her mother's arms,
She can regard skeletons and spiders with a chuckle.
She is safe from goblins, elves and all the scary things
of the world.

3. Visitors (Aged 3)

She has been busy all evening
Upstaging her siblings,
Dancing, pirouetting,
Flouncing, singing,
Flattering with kisses.

But now,
Her head falls wearily
Across her father's shoulder
And, against her utmost will,
She sleeps.

Cousins: Jake at Four and a Half, Sophie at Three

You are running still around my head when I wake —
Laughing through doors,
Breaking out into the green garden.

Then suddenly again you are quiet,
And I find you have made a house under the table
With chairs for walls.

And when I look beneath,
You are leafing through books,
Chatting contentedly

Like and old couple
Across a fire
In the Sabbath of their years.

Chameleon

· Jake at 5

You were telling me, with wide-eyed earnestness,
About how you climbed the tree
And never noticed a jutting sprig
Until you scratched your finger against it
And cut yourself sorely.

Then, as I bent to better see the scar,
I noted a burst of brightness in your face
As you grabbed the phone from my pocket
And scooted down the garden, laughing,
My aging limbs in hot pursuit.

Liam, at Three and a Half

Never was there one
Surrounded so by love;
And, bit by bit,
We watch its drip-drip
Breach your carapace.

A year ago,
You dodged your mother's eyes;
But now you seek them out,
As you splash and chuckle
In a watery wonderworld.

There are times still
When you retire
Behind stockades we can't traverse;
But a turning doorkey
Summons you back;

And, as your father lifts
And tips you to the sky,
Your laughter lights
Every cobwebbed corner
Of our hearts.

* My wonderful grandnephew, Liam,
  is on the autistic spectrum.

Our Liam

He finds our banter baffling,
Cannot read our faces or our moods.

Information is a hail of pummelling rocks
And he must turn within to shelter from it.

When he speaks, the words that come
Are not the words he needs to say.

Change is agony, the unexpected, crucifixion:
He screams and stomps and cannot tell us why.

Delightedly he watches as his cousins play
But cannot think how he might join.

He is at home in water
Or jumping on a mattress up and down

Or bolting terrifyingly down a hill,
Thrilled by the feel of his own running feet.

He spends hours choosing shapes for spaces, lining things in rows,
Watching a video where the same thing always happens over.

Lounging with his granddad on a couch,
He throws himself all at once across him,

Rubbing his face against a jumper's softness,
Stroking with delight the grandpaternal stubble.

And there are times too when the very bliss of being
    transports him
To rapturous realms our spancilled senses never reach.

Liam Arís

He is that waiter in the bar in France,
Without the language.

Sometimes through guess or intuition
Or ferreting through the pictures in his mind,

He gets the orders pat.
Sometimes he fails and every face around is frowning.

Now and again our ordinary is so impossible
That he must stop the world and scream.

Oisín at 6

Streetlamps pale into dawn.
I drive by your house,
Straight from a hospice ward,
And think of you
In the heavy warmth of your room,
Your comfort-blanket fallen from your fingers:

And pray a bright angel to visit you in your dreams,
Telling you how deeply loved you are
In your earnestness,
Your tripping-excitedly-over-words-iness,
Your joy in being in the world:
For all the shining self of you.

Lisbon

for Karl and Joana on their wedding eve

You have brought us from our ordinary
Into these shaded alleys, where strong sun cannot burn
And old women sit all day on steps,
Shelling peas and guarding children's play;

Onto squares, where fountains gush and splash,
Sacraments of earth's incessant flux;
Through the Summer palaces of weary kings,
Tiled anterooms, secret courtyards with orangetrees
        and swans;

To this seafront,
Where we stroll at evening,
While lorries pass above us on a bridge,
Blessed by a pitying Christ.

May you too
Have pity in your love,
Ebullience of water,
Shade from burning sun.

Love is Like

for Mary and Nick on their wedding day

Love is like the trees in the wild orchard
That twist and turn and purl together

Till two together,
Through wind and shine and seasons' buffeting,
Grow to a single thing

That fills the Summer sky with blossom
And weighs the Autumn down with apples.

February Morning

That morning, a woman I admire
Told me she must die:
All the doctors offered was an easy passing.

She was preparing vegetables by a window,
A hill behind her, winter-brown;
A cloud descending, laden with rain.

In a corner of neglected lawn,
I saw fresh primroses, faces
Amazed by their entrance into light.

Prayer in Age

Let me trust You, Lord, to the going-out of my days.

When I am led again in halterstrings,
Grant that I be led kindly:
Do not abandon me to derision.

When nights are dark
And I have no strength, even to pray,
Do not cast me off.

Lead me to those fields
Where every sheep is known by name.
Let me be as rain on Your ocean.

Fin

Walking through woods,
You come suddenly upon the lake,
Its length and spread taking away your breath.

A haze hangs over it.
Two swans move in the shallows.
There is a jetty far across under beeches.

A boat moves towards you on placid water:
Trust and embark!

Laying Out

They lay her out in the front room,
Perfumed candles burning quietly beside her,
Flowers on a table, a photograph showing her waving.

They have dressed her in the suit she wore to the last wedding,
A blouse with ruches,
A necklace she loved.

Somebody has rubbed creams on her face,
Combed dye into her hair,
Pencilled in her brows, dusted her off with powder.

People come in, fall silent,
Remark on how beautiful she looks,
As if that had something to say to anything.

Vita Brevis

for Baby Niamh O'Malley

We knew you only for a single day
And blessed you with water
And gave you a name;

And though your going broke
And breaks us still,
We treasure every turn and twist you gave

And thank God,
Even in our pain,
That once we held you fast.

Gonzaga

Weeks have passed
Since our stiff and holy commendations:
I come now for my own farewell
And find brambles by your grave,
Full of fruit.

Bees swarm busily on lavender,
A pheasant crosses my path
Like the ones who came,
Then vanished (screeching),
In your childhood fields:

And in the overgrowth
By the river,
A host of butterflies
Flutters
In lovely disarray.

Nun

in memory of Sr. Gonzaga Clancy C.H.F. 1922–2012

No one has dead-headed the roses this Autumn
And no one is sure who will make the Christmas cakes.
No one knows who to call if a slate falls from the roof,
Or chutes collapse under snow, or the boiler judders to a stop.

There will be no one now returning from town
With a hundred tales garnered on buses.
Who else, at ninety, will charm the tyro docs,
Create a flutter among the waiters in the grimmest restaurant?

Who will make soup for the beggar at the gate,
Butter *a son gout* his sandwiches?
Who will make chance into occasion,
Turn drab days into festival?

Who will we treasure our odd encounters for, to draw her
      laughter?
Who will remember the names we forget?
If we tell tales of her now, they will be edged with sadness:
We will be chuckling; and hiding tears.

Seven Alone

1. WIDOWER

He comes each day to the same restaurant,
Eats the same meal,
Feels the loss as if it were yesterday.

The waitresses flirt gently with him.
The regulars stop to talk of football, funerals,
The great affairs of state,

He leaves when he has done,
Carrying his loneliness.

2. WIDOW

Whenever she goes to the old village,
She brings back the unsweetened biscuits her husband loved.
She has a special jar so they are always fresh.

They are perfect with wine or milk
As she sits, waiting for night to fall,
Going back over sorrows and infected joys.

3. WIDOWER

He dreamt of bringing her,
When she had settled,
For walks in the park near the Home.

He would watch her watch gleefully
The children at their play,
Draw enchantment from the notes of meadow-birds.

They would walk hand in hand beneath the beeches,
Planted an unremembered time ago
By someone, like him, with hope.

4. WIDOW

Her nephew meets her at the station in his rickety car.
His daughters, delighting in her odd glamour,
Carry her cases into the hotel.
She kisses them warmly when they leave.
She asks for a tranquil room,
Where she can lie long in the afternoon,
Listening to crickets.

As days pass, she will call on friends,
Stroll into churches,
Visit shops, make small purchases.
She will walk on the sea wall
Above the anchored boats,
Watch sprats lead mackerel to shore,
Aware of how tiny our place is in the world.

5. WIDOWER

Somewhere upriver there has been a great rain
And the waters are full again.

He sits on his bench,
Withdrawn from all that might ever again touch him,

Deaf to the elation of songbirds,
Whoops of children,

Hurdy-gurdy of the ice-cream van,
Slish-slosh of a river.

6. WIDOW

She kisses his photograph
Before she climbs the stairs
At evening,

Holding no bitterness
Though he has left her
To face old age alone.

7. WIDOWER

They gather at the door,
Spread themselves around the garden in the cold,
Waiting for the coffin.

He looks all his eighty years,
Watching the hearse align with the gateposts.
The children draw close to comfort him.

He knows his own end is near.
He prays it may be soon.

House

No one has lived in the house since they died.
Early on, somebody came for the chairs, the oak sideboard.
For a time, the geraniums kept blossoming.

Now the curtains disintegrate,
The windowframes collapse,
The clay hardens in the pots.

Progress

The bulldozers have come
To knock the walls dividing the fields.
Ancient roads fall before them,
Abandoned houses,
Shortcuts across the land.

No memory will stay of the old connections:
Spring wells, landmark rocks,
Bail-ó-Dhias annso isteach.
The paths and maps are in our minds
And we will be gone.

The Dún of Eogan Bél

from the Irish, 13th century

Behold Eogan's fort above the lake
Where hordes of warriors were slain!
Eogan himself no longer thrives:
The fort above the lake survives.

The place where Eogan's corpse was waked,
The house he built, still remains.
The queen with whom he shared his bed,
Like Eogan himself, is dead.

Savage he was who owned this house,
Ravaging Ireland, North and South.
Unlucky they whose tax was out:
He hung thirty liegemen for a cow.

He scourged the Liffey countryside,
Laid Munster low thirty times.
There wasn't in all the land
A tribe he did not challenge.

He forayed into Munster
To gather gold and plunder.
To swell his hoard of precious gems,
He took hostages of upright men.

A third of his force he sent
Beyond Luachair to Brandon Head.
Another third he ordered off
To Kenmare of the Scholars.

He himself, at Druimm Abrat,
With a further third, caused ruin and rack.
Laying Munster low was sport
To Eogan and that darling force.

But now we see his heirs rise up:
Nettles, weeds of every sort.
For all the wealth that he possessed,
Such now is his lineage.

Quatrains from the Irish

19th Century

1.

At morning or at noon?
On sea or on land?
I know my death must come.
Alas to know not when!

2.

None of the generations survives
Of all of them, back to Adam.
For myself, I do not know
If I have any tomorrow.

3.

My bed is prepared,
A narrow bed in cold earth,
Me lying on those before,
Others lined to lie atop me.

4.

I never met a wise one yet
Who knew the way the crowds went,
Who died since all was first begotten.
Alas that swiftly we must follow!

5.

This earth on which I stand
Will one day be heaped upon me.
I'm above the ground for now.
Tomorrow it will be atop me.

6.

O how this loneliness afflicts me
On a cold bed, no sheet beneath me,
The shovel pitching clay at my eye,
The mourners readying to retire!

7.

You who crookedly build up your stock,
Don't you notice how swiftly life passes on?
Alexander, who conquered the world in a flash,
Has no more ground now than any poor man.

Johannine Epilogue

We were in a small inlet.
Water sloshed against shingle.
Day was failing.

Two swans moved by a grey wall.
A seagull called.
Lights came on on a far quayside.

There was a circle of charred sticks
On the shore.
A boat came home, heavy with fish.

Incarnation

for JFD

1.

We would have done it otherwise:

We would have kept the fluttering messengers,
The journey in haste,
The wondrous birth.

Pity is important;
So we would have allowed him pain
And pity.

We would have kept the feasting,
The sinner companions,
The softness of God.

But what need was there
For the garden agony, the nails through the palms,
The roars from the cross?

2.

Feeling as men and women feel,
Quaking before pain
As men and women quake,

He entrusts Himself to the High Father
As men and women trust themselves
To human constancy;

And, trusting still that luminous love,
He edges on
To the blind halt of death.

3.

That all of this — sun, water's rush,
Men and women moving, haloed, through the streets —
Came from nothing, nowhere, nobody,
I cannot credit; so believe.

It is afterwards I baulk:
Mind-melting-Otherness?
Or Otherness-Made-Flesh,
Softly among us?

4.

And, being man,

Did he think, as men and women thought,
That Jonah dwelt three days within the whale,
Immune to belly juices?

That devils lived flamboyantly inside the sick
And, when his heart was moved to heal,
Left them, yelping?

That the world soon,
With hail and lightening bolt,
Must end?

How did he foresee
The horror of his dying,
The direful future of Jerusalem?

And how much grasp unknowable God,
Bending in his flesh
To pitch among us?

5.

Jn. 15, 9-11

With human arms
Grappling each of us to human heart,
There stilling us,

The love that flows from Father-God,
And all God's joy,
Holds each of us, through Him,

In an embrace,
Where each of us
Is marvellous and singular,

Where there is no longer need
For talk or explanation, gestures of regret;
Just simple surrender to our God's delight.

6.

Eyes closed tenderly by others,
Open into the gloom.
Limbs stir,

He stands,
Laughing in the joy of newness.

Light comes through the entry.
Morning birds are singing.
His heart is full.
Love has proved true.
He moves to meet the women in the sun.

.

Passover

All across the city,
The fevered bleating of lambs;
And, then, the noises of slaughter!

Blood everywhere — in halls, in kitchens,
On doors, on lintels,
Spattered over the people!

And so they lead him,
Spancilled animal,
Into the gore.

Blinded

After all the years of holding up the bread,
Calling attention to the presence,
After all the years of welcoming the freshly fledged
Beneath Your shelter,

After all the years of listening in Your stead
To chronicles of wrong,
Offering comprehension,
And years of pleas for wisdom, healing,

After years of digging through
The arguments of Palestine,
Presenting, astonished over,
Those parables of joy,

After all the years of reaching in Your name
To sick and halt, the dying and the dead,
Your Godness blinds me yet
To Who You are.

Synagogue

Mark 6, 1–6

In green clearings where crickets beat their wings
And lizards run at lightspeed over stones,
We find You easily;

Or when we watch the ocean break on rocks,
Or look on fish disporting in brightwater coves,
Or walk on sands.

But how can we admit You, come,
Simple and a man,
Stood in the assembly, reading from the scroll.

A Christmas Poem

No longer able to believe
That the Great Unknowable
Came among us as a child,

He finds a way,
This tinselly time of year,
To the crib and the singing,

In some kind of fealty
To those whose softness
Nourished his growing;

And, for a moment,
Dreams himself back
Into the sweetness.

Mary

If she had said 'No',
The world would not have stopped:
Birds would have flown high still into sky,
The heavens would have proclaimed His glory
And the firmament the work of His hands.

We would have gone on reproving Him,
Unaware of how deeply down
His love might plunge into our affliction,
Unaware of how He might have taken upon Himself
The consequences of our 'Nos'.

Crucifixes

Over time,
They forgot the emaciated limbs,
The sinuous twist of Moses' serpent on a stick,

Casting him in gold,
With floating draperies around his loins
And jolly cherubs at his shins,

Beautiful enough
To grace the bedroom
Of any strumpet queen.

Holding Away The Dark

"Fiche bliain ag fás,
Fiche bliain ag borradh 'sag at,
Fiche bliain ag titim,
Fiche bliain cuma tú ann nó as".
— *Traidisiúnta, Déisibh Mumhan*

1.

Dead leaves scrape across the paving of the derelict church.
A small crowd is gathered with candles.
A priest sits by a white-clothed table.
How long more can we hold away the dark?

2.

We hang onto the inherited dream
Like ageing, disappointed lovers,
Left in the end
With nowhere else to go.

3.

Have mercy on us, Lord,
Who have lived beyond our time of usefulness
And totter round the empty edifices of our glory,
Looking towards our end.

4

.

The rigid will inherit the earth;
And we, who knew You gentle,
Comprehending of failure, soft on offence,
Will fade, forgotten, from the world.

5.

Yet we persist
Like that small bird of dawn
Cheeping cussedly
In the chorus of the forest.

6.

Infants ail, mothers weep, fathers bury sons.
Those without hope look to us for hope, who have no hope;
But call from some willed, neglected corner of our selves,
To an unfelt God, for succour.

7.

A door opens,
A door closes.
One by one, we enter the place of prayer,
Carrying our unfaith.

8.

We sit through the Lauds,
Minds linking no longer with the words,
Feeling neither Presence nor Absence,
Mouthing the pleadings blankly.

9.

We paw the dark windows of Otherness,
Hoping for a shaft of atactile light
To pass across us
Momentarily.

10.

In our lives now, no songbird sings, no mouse makes rustle.
We exist merely,
Trusting, against wisdom, in that footfall promised
That once in Galilee moved on water.

Friars at Prayer

We gather for the regulation hours,
Pleading savagely beneath our calm,
For nurture,

Clustered,
Like the waving mouths of corals,
Gathering floating plankton from the water,

Or like scalds in a nest,
Opening wide their throats in hunger;
And though we cheep

And hear the other's needier cheeping,
None of us knows, unless You teach,
How to reach and comfort.

Pobal Dé

They come for weddings, christenings, funerals,
Carrying slivers of wishing-to-believe.

I stand, with quivering faith,
Gathering their hardly-prayer,

Knowing how halting is the flame
That spurts from logic-dampened fires,

Knowing how ersatz gods at every turn beguile us,
Willing an Easter joy to burst across the earth to madden them.

The Olive Garden

1.

Shoots sprout green on gnarled branches,
Songbirds flirt with feathered paramours,
Lovers walk out under trees:

That my life, even in age, may have truth,
I must step away from all this burgeoning,
Go resolutely to the Olive Garden.

2.

A fly moves along my arm,
Sifting the hairs.
The world is full of sorrow.
She alone shows me tenderness.

3.

Watching how smoothly the flood flows over a tiny fall,
I pray to be touched; and touched tenderly.
My body cries for succouring
And You, Lord, are all I have.

Park

The beeches are unashamed,
Posing nude
In unseasonal November sunlight.

The ducks have multiplied on the pond.
Seagulls have vanished to the cliffs.
The river rushes to be off.

People go by with dogs.
Joggers jog,
Tennis balls pip pop.

The mountains look benignly on us,
Caught in the round and round
Of our unGodded world.

God in Winter

1.

We have exhausted ourselves doing good,
Building our infected kingdom,
And have wept to see the tempests take it.

Now we lay our burden down
And wait for You,
Who have been tending elsewhere,

To stun us in the wilderness
With sudden shoots.

2.

As when the sun on a bleak day
Makes its somehow way
Through an overhang of trees
Onto a river
And the swift race dances onward,
Splotched with gold,

So, in grey weathers,
Your mirthful manifesting.

3.

In the hush when the bread has been shared
And the shuffle back to pews has stopped
And the choir is silent for a time:
The rustle of divinity.

Consubstantial

We do not need to believe
The stories of kings and shepherds,
Choirs and messengers,

Though they tell us better
Than the metaphors of our creeds
That He who is above all

Has plunged Himself,
Out of love,
Into our commonplace.

Ramparts

First, the ramparts;
Then, below the ramparts,
The ever-in-and-out of the sea!

A gull cries.
Somebody in the distance plucks strings.
Behind us, the town falls back towards the hills.

Men come from doorways
With effigies of the tortured Saviour.
People kneel in the streets, sing rawthroated songs.

Out on the inhospitable rocks, a gannet drifts onto sky.

Weathers

1.

Kingfishers fall famished to the earth.
The lake is locked in ice;
The river's flow is stopped.
A stag moves out from the trees,
Shaking snow from branches.

A thrush and robin quarrel:
A pampered cat waits in shadow.

2.

From our safe shelters,
We watch the rains
Create pools in the grasses,
Obscure the hills,
Become one with the sea.

Not for us an early rising
To tend to soaking lambs,
Drive cows into byres for milking!
Not for us the grief as stalks bend and fall
Before a heartless pounding.

Festival

Behind the stalls, the bulbs on strings,
The children circling, laughing,
On the roundabouts,
The unfeeling sea moves across stones.

The Young

1.

Having achieved all the futures we dreamed of,
They move into the houses of the dead,
Adding glass rooms, bespoke kitchens,
As if there were permanence.

2.

Like snuff
From the fingers of shawlies in snugs,
Our cherished wisdoms
Slip from their fingers.

Retreat

I left the leaping horses behind,
The vivid tents, the race of water,

The fathers taking photographs,
The mothers, after the ordeal, gasping for tea,

The sons jostling,
The girls, in billowing frocks, laughing across a bridge;

And found a way uphill
To a green square, where the gentle old

Gather in shafts of dying sun.

Place

Sitting before a great cathedral,
Letting my eye move up along the stone
In the last of the sunlight,

Watching pigeons find their niches,
Small birds drop for crumbs,
A dog twist, lazy-bellied, on the steps,

I am certain still
That every drifting mote has place;
And we are gathered all

In the upswell of Benevolence.